BETWEEN THE MOUNTAINS

Between the Mountains

Poems from Big Valley

ROY DAVID KANAGY

SANTOS BOOKS

EVERY STORY SACRED

ISBN: 979-8-9936553-0-7
Published by Santos Books LLC, Elizabethtown, PA
Conrad L. Kanagy, CEO and Executive Publisher
First Printing, 2025

Contents

Foreword

Growing up in Belleville, Pennsylvania, in the heart of Big Valley, Roy Kanagy cherished his family, worked diligently, and enjoyed casting a fishing line into Kishacoquillas Creek. Over 59 years, I had the privilege of knowing him as my dad, and in that time I gained insight into his passions and inclinations, which are reflected throughout the following pages of poetry. As you read on, you will gain a deeper understanding of his family, work, hobbies, Big Valley, and his love and devotion to Jesus Christ. I was constantly impressed by his quick wit and readiness to share a rhyme or excerpt from a poem he had written.

Even in his final days, he continued to share meaningful words that flowed together in poetry. On one occasion, while in rehabilitation over Valentine's Day, an aide asked the residents about the meaning of love, and Dad responded with an excerpt from his "Happy Valentine's Day" poem:

Love is more than Cupid's bow,
Shooting arrows, as we know,
Though romance plays a vital part
In winning over someone's heart!

Love is sharing a lovely smile,
Love is going the second mile.
Love is helping someone in need,
Love is sharing instead of greed...

This book of poetry was something Mom always wanted to see come to pass. And though Dad and Mom are now with Jesus, my siblings and I are blessed to see Mom's dream come true. If you appreciate poetry, you will enjoy the diverse thoughts expressed in rhyme, and in the process, learn about the life of a humble man who was born, raised, found love and married, had four children, and many grandchildren all while living a simple life in rural, Pennsylvania, and just maybe you will be inspired to write your life's story in rhyme as well.

Curtiss Kanagy, 2025

Christmas

MARY'S LULLABY

In a manger a baby cries
While Mary sings a lullaby
Softly soothing baby's fears
Are the words the baby hears.

All around the world today
Amid society's decay
That lullaby still is heard
Bringing peace with every word.

Christ gives hearts sweet release
With his words of love and peace
That lullaby still fills the air
As we live, love and share!

THE GLORY OF CHRISTMAS

The sunset shows God's glory
Then slips into the night.
The moon responses accordingly
To give the heaven light.
So in the darkness of the night
God's glory was made known.
To shepherds caring for their sheep,
It came from heaven's throne.
Christ is born in Bethlehem
The shepherds went to see,
The glory of the Christ child
Born to set us free!
His glory never fades away
His words bring sweet release,
Have a blessed Christmas
May His glory bring you peace!

THE LIGHTS OF CHRISTMAS

The lights of Christmas are everywhere
Lighting up the cool night air.
It's Christmas time!

Their radiant glow floods the land
As hearts unite, peace extends its hand
To catch their beauty.

They invite us to the manger
To welcome Jesus, that lovely stranger
Who gives us light.

The lights of Christmas never dim
If we give our hearts to Him.
Jesus is light and love!

THE LIGHT IN THE STABLE

In a stable in Bethlehem one dark night
God in heaven turned on the light.
The light went unnoticed till the heavens were filled
With angels telling shepherds out in the field.

Their message was, "Go, go and see
For this light from heaven will set you free!"
True was the message for there they saw
The light of the world asleep on the straw.

A star in the East brought Wise Men to see
This wonderful savior, the Messiah to be.
Prophets had spoken, "When the time was right
A light would shine in their darkest night."

We as the angels have a message that frees us,
"The light of the world is the baby called Jesus."
We, as the star in the heavens so bright,
Lead people to Jesus in life's darkest night!
(Matthew 5:14)

COME TO THE MANGER
(SONG)

Come to the manger, Jesus is here.
Come to the manger, you need not fear.
Come to the manger, heaven will cheer.
Joy will surround you, God's love is here.

Come to the manger if you have a need.
Here at the manger your soul is freed.
Come to the manger, heaven you've found.
Angels and glory are all around.

Here in the manger a baby cries
Mary is singing lu –lu –abies.
Here in the manger a baby sleeps,
Joseph is thinking thoughts that are deep.

Refrain:

If you come with the Wise men, follow the star.
If you come with the shepherds, come as you are.
If you come with a friend or even a foe,
Bow down and worship before you go.

THE GIFTS OF CHRISTMAS

Beneath the Christmas tree there lies
Packages that hold surprise
For young and old with wondering eyes.

Some would sneak and take a peak
Shake and rattle so to speak
For curiosity makes them weak.

So the gift of CHRISTMAS lies
In a MANGER, what a surprise
In SWADDLING CLOTHES before our eyes!

The SHEPHERDS could hardly wait to see
And WISE MEN everywhere agree
This gift was sent to set us free.

May the gifts of CHRISTMAS always bring
You, PEACE and LOVE in everything
With JOY that makes the ANGELS sing!

THE INN WAS "OUT" OF ROOM

Each heart is an inn
Where Jesus would live,
Each heart could be blessed
By the gift He would give.

The gift of Salvation
Deliverance from sin,
But many are "out"
When Jesus wants in.

Each Christmas we rejoice
For God's gift from above,
And share many gifts
With those who we love.

But the rest of the year
We often can't win,
Because we are "out"
When Jesus wants in.

This Christmas respond
When He knocks on the door,
For He will return
Though He has been there before.

He bears a gift
Salvation from sin,

Make sure you're not "out"
When Jesus wants in.

Bethlehem's Inn was full!
There's no doubt,
They missed a great blessing
Because they were "out."

A STABLE PEACE

It's Christmastime and once again
We hear the wondrous story,
How Christ was born in Bethlehem
In a stable without glory.

The angels announced the blessed news
As the shepherds shook with fright.
The night was lit up as the day
The glory was so bright.

The shepherds went to Bethlehem
To see this child so tender.
There they worshipped Christ, the Lord
In a stable without splendor.

The Wise men came to give him gifts
Three kinds of great renown.
They bowed down in the stable bare,
On that most kings would frown.

Christ is the Savior of the world.
His kingdom will increase,
Still the world is looking for
The key to heaven's peace.

Peace does not come from Washington
Or start in Moscow's Square.
Peace does not come with lots of oil
Or the money that we share.

Peace does not come from M.X. Missiles
Hid beneath the ground.
Peace does not come with fast airplanes
That break the speed of sound.

Peace comes today as it did then
In humility it starts;
As we bow and worship Him in the stable,
The stable of our hearts.

THE CHRISTMAS GIFT

God gave us a gift on Christmas Day,
A special gift he sent our way.
That gift was Jesus Christ our Lord,
A gift that everyone can afford.

Ten lepers found that gift one day.
They were healed and sent on their way.
The blind man found that gift so free.
He was healed and he could see.

A man possessed by the demons throng
Could not be held, he was so strong.
Found healing for his heart and soul,
Jesus freed him and made him whole.

Lazarus, a friend of Jesus, whom
Died and lay inside his tomb,
Was given back his life we know.
Jesus said, "Free him and let him go."

One of the thieves on Calvary,
Paying for his wrongs in his misery
Asked for mercy as he paid the price.
Jesus took him to paradise.

Again some day he will appear
To lift the curse of death and fear.
Then we'll celebrate in heaven's way
The gift of God on Christmas Day!

THE CHRISTMAS STAR

It shone one night
Over Bethlehem.
It shone so bright
Wise men came.

It shines today
Over the world.
In a special way
On the face of Christ

Wise men still
Detect its glow.
Wise men will
Follow Christ

THE WONDERS OF CHRISTMAS

Many wondered at the birth of Christ
The Messiah, God's only Son.
Many failed to understand
The mission of the Holy One.

Mary wondered when the angel came
And told her it was she
Who would be the mother of the One
To come from eternity.

Joseph wondered when he heard
And thought her to be untrue,
Until it was revealed to him,
Exactly what to do.

The shepherds wondered at the sight
Of angels in the night,
And wondered at the words they spoke
As they shook with fright.

The wise men wondered at the star,
The star that shone so bright,
They followed it until it stopped
Over Bethlehem that night.

Today we wonder at His love,
That miracle of yore
But wise men everywhere now know
What he came here for.

He said He will return
And take us all to glory,
Then we'll understand at last
Heaven's great love story.

A HOLY CHILD

We love you, Little Baby
Asleep upon the straw.
You are the Savior of the world.
You love us one and all.

Your dimples are so beautiful,
Your cheeks a rosy red.
It seems there is a special glow
That rests upon your head.

You lie there so contentedly
Upon the cattle's straw.
It seems you do not even mind
The way the cattle bawl.

Your manger bed is quite unfit
For a babe who is a King,
For one who came from glory
Where the angels sing.

By the look of satisfaction
That we see upon your face,
We know for sure that we can rest
Upon your saving grace.

For you have brought us heaven's love
By coming down to earth,
And made a way to heaven for those
Who experience a new birth.

Creation

SPRING

The warming of the sun's bright rays
The gradual lengthening of the days
We look for Spring!
The melting snow and slippery ice
Watch your step is good advice
We look for Spring!
We don't have winters like years ago
But this one's close I think you know
We look for Spring.
We're hoping that the robin's song
Will be heard before too long
Praise God for SPRING!!!!

THE MOUNTAIN

The mountain stands so proud and tall
Just beyond the garden wall.
It rises swiftly as if to salute
The valley laden with its fruit.

The mass of dirt, rocks and trees
Whisper softly in the breeze.
And though their words entice me much
It is the silence that holds me in its clutch!

It stands a monument to God
This mass of trees, rocks and sod.
The people in the valley share
The strength and beauty God put there.

It stands a refuge proud and tall
For the wild turkeys as they call.
The deer, squirrel and bear when chased
Find refuge in its strong embrace.

The mountain gives refreshment and rest.
In its woods the soul is blest.
From its rock the waters splash
Resounding with a gentle crash.

When God pulls the shades of night
He'll set the sun with glory bright.
Upon the mountains top to show
His glory to the earth below.

The mountain stands so proud and tall
Just beyond the garden wall.
God calls each of us to share
A mountaintop experience there.

THE CORNFIELDS

The cornstalks stand
Across Big Valley's fields
With arms upraised they worship God
And promise him their yield.

Their tassels acknowledge
All his wondrous ways
They whisper of his love and grace
Giving heaven praise.

With their ears
They listen for commands
Knowing that they give their lives
To honor man's demands.

Unselfishly they fall
Bowing to his will
Giving their lives and fruit in pain
As the corn bins fill.

God is satisfied
He'll honor them indeed
Once again next spring with love
He'll resurrect their seed!

HILLTOPS

The valleys of life
Mostly unknown
Produce a sigh,
A moan or a groan.

The hilltops are brighter
A treasure the view
The clouds float along
In a sea of pure blue.

The breeze is a pleasure
Refreshing and cool
The soul is refreshed
As it bathes in its pool.

Down in the valley
With its forest of sorrow
One soon could forget
The joy of tomorrow.

The hilltop is still there
When you cannot grin
The difference is only
The position you're in!

THE BUFFALO

A wonderful beast is the buffalo,
It roamed the earth a long time ago.
The Indians hunted it for its meat.
Its flesh was very good to eat.
They used its fur to keep them warm,
For with winter came the wind and the storm.
Man took advantage of this beast.
Its presence on earth almost ceased.
But its spirit still thrives in the hearts of men,
Who take advantage of you if they can.
And stomp your flesh into the ground,
So no one knows that you're around.
Be very careful as you travel life's road,
Or you just might be "Buffaloed."

O LOVELY TREES

I welcome Autumn with its lovely sights,
I wait and watch the trees, until the time is right,
When God, with all His power and His might,
Will paint them lovely colors in the night.
For God will change their lush green summer clothes,
And in their pretty nightgowns they will pose,
Awaiting sleep.
A sleep restful and deep.

But winter soon will deal them serious blows
And swiftly strip them of their lovely clothes.
Then they will stand naked, bleak, stark,
Dressed only in their skin, the bark.
Yet still with arms and hands upraised
They will give unto their maker glorious praise.
And God will honor them in their repose,
And cover them again, this time with lovely snows.

With freezing rain and ice,
Once again they will be beautiful and nice.
O lovely trees, I'll see you in the spring,
When once again I'll hear the robin sing.
When once again I'll see you dressed supreme,
Arrayed in many, many lovely shades of green.
Now as the sunset slips into the night, or so it seems,
I wish you many, many pleasant dreams.

SPRINGTIME SPLENDOR

I watched God spread His carpet out
so green upon the lawn.
I watched Him warming up the frost
until it all was gone.
I watched Him push the tulips up
and rouse the bumble bee.
I watched Him as He placed the robin
back up in the tree.
I watched Him as He painted
all the trees a lovely green.
I watched Him send the gentle showers
so refreshing and so clean.
Only God in His wisdom, His power
and His might,
Could recreate this scene each Spring
and have it come out right.

SPRING TO LIFE

Springtime fills the earth with awe
As the ice begins to thaw.

The sunshine reaches out its arm
Touching earth with warmth and charm.

The daffodil breaks through to see
If the sun has set it free.

Flocks of geese fly in the air
Robins are seen everywhere.

Springtime has its special ways
Of filling up the earth with praise.

The God of heaven shows perfection
Each spring he gives us resurrection!

THE MIGHTY WIND

Oh, mighty wind, I'd like to know,
Where do you come from, where do you go?
When you are blowing, your strength is known,
By the things you do, your might is shown.
You cause us people so much woe
As over the land you wildly blow.
You cause the captains on ships to curse,
As you turn up your volume from bad to worse.
You even cancel the airplane's flight.
Because of your power and your might!
You travel so fast to the earth's far ends,
You pick tornadoes for your friends.
The dark black clouds and the hurricanes,
Are often mentioned with your name.

Then the wind did howl and roar,

"Oh, mister man, I do deplore
You always look on the dark side of me,
There's a better side you do not see!
I put the twinkle in the little boy's eye,
As I toss his kite high in the sky.
I display the beauty of the maiden fair.
As I gently ripple through her hair.
I turn the windmill 'round and 'round.
Pumping the water out of the ground!
After the rain and after the flood,
I come along and dry up the mud.

The smog and fog you need not fear,
For I will make them disappear.
Don't you see the people smile,
As I push their sailboat mile after mile?
On a hot summer's night I come disguised,
As a cooling breeze as the temperatures rise.
Oh, mister man, do not despair,
For I travel the earth without a care.
But where I come from and where I go,
Oh, mister man, you'll never know!!" John 3:8

SPRING DOUBTS

Winter is back,
The geese have flew.
The robins,
Don't know what to do!
Winds are strong,
The snow a slew.
The people,
Don't know what to do!
Clouds soon pass,
What a blew.
The sunshine
Still knows what to do!

CRAFTY INDIAN

Crafty Indian go on a hunt,
Get out call and grunt and grunt.

Finally call him in big doe,
Bring it home and have big show.

Archery season still not done,
Him go out to have more fun!

Him now skilled to shoot 'em buck,
But seems him have rotten luck.

Though him crafty as can be,
Seems him always hit 'em tree.

Last day of season him in luck,
Shoot 'em down an eight-point buck!

Him come home with great big smile
Call in family for big Pow-wow!

Family take look and all agree,
Great Spirit keep arrow from hitting tree!!

WINTER CHOICES

I never chose the winter snows
To lie beneath my feet.
Nor chose the wind to rattle the tin
While I was fast asleep.

But I will choose to enjoy the views
The landscape painted white.
Each day it lies beneath my feet
I'll make it my delight.

I never chose the wind's harsh blows
To knock me off my feet.
Nor chose the ice so slippery and nice
To act as a comfortable seat.

But I will choose to take a snooze
In comfort on my chair.
Then of the ice and howling wind
I will not be aware.

I never chose as furious foes
Those little folks so dear.
Nor chose the snowballs as they fall
To hit me on the rear.

But I will choose to change my shoes
And go out in the snow.
I'll make some snowballs of my own

And conquer every foe.

I never chose the slippery roads
To cause my car to slide.
Nor chose "my dear" to shriek in fear,
"You're going to hit the side!"

But I will choose while on a cruise
To slide the car a bit.
But when "my dear" begins to shriek
I'll know I had better quit.

Yes, winter comes and winter goes.
Its choices quite unclear.
You might as well enjoy it, friends,
For it comes every year.

Big Valley

NEW HOLLAND'S BELLEVILLE PLANT

Between the mountains in Central PA
A New Holland plant is working today.
Neatly tucked in the Valley of Kish.
Many a farmer may find their wish!
Here you can hear the engine's roar
As skid steer loaders move out of the door.
A new paint system is part of the pace
As workers respond to the industry's race.
Technology fills the worker's desire
As lasers respond with tongues of fire.
As you watch you will notice that
They aren't building a "Kitty Cat!"
So if your skid steer jumps and jerks
Try one of theirs and see how it works.

Between the mountains in Central PA,
A New Holland Plant is working today
In a little town a bit out of your way.
This little town is Belleville, PA.

THE KISHACOQUILLAS VALLEY

There is a land, a valley called Kish
A land for which many a person might wish.
With lush green meadows, peaceful and still
Cows out grazing as they will.

Here, my friend, on a summer day
You'll enjoy the smell of drying hay.
You'll enjoy the sight of the golden grain
Bowing and swaying with the wind and in.

Here the mountain and the stream
Fulfill the hunter and the fisherman's dream.
The stream refreshes man and beast
For without water, life would cease.

Contented people here are found.
They use horses to work the ground.
Often we hear the clip clop sound
Of horses' shoes upon the ground.

The Amish buggies, what a sight!
Like giant fireflies, they light up the night.
O, what contentment, what glorious bliss
To live within the Valley of Kish!

Here at times you can hear
Voices singing loud and clear,
A neighbor's voice as he tills the sod
Or Amish young folks praising God.

In the Fall, the leaves on the trees
Change to bright colors and sway in the breeze.
The beauty of nature is shown so clear
The glory of God is shown here.

No, it's not Las Vegas, and it's not like Texas,
Though money and oil at times do affect us.
But it's very possible if many had their wish,
They would choose to live in the Valley of Kish!

THE ROAR OF SILENCE IN BELLEVILLE

At an N.H. Plant on the banks of a stream
Many came for a job as part of life's dream.
Becoming a part of a company that everyone said
Would decorate the world with yellow and red!

In a humble beginning, Hertzler and Zook
Wrote the first chapter in its history book.
And how it expanded throughout the years
Brought jubilation and many loud cheers!

Competitors came; we built their machines
For quality walked on the banks of this stream.
Bringing life to production and harvesting yields
For the farmers "outstanding" in their many fields.

Soon the buildings are empty, the workers all gone.
The air tools no longer will be singing their song.
No engines will be heard in the night or the dawn
The parking lots too, as bare as the lawn.

Already silence is walking the floors
Locks keep hands from opening doors.
What will the voices of history bring
To a silence so loud you can't hear a thing?

THE BELLEVILLE OUTHOUSE

Through the years the outhouse stood
Crude and without perfection
But if you had to go, it was at best
A move in the right direction.
The septic tank was better still
The indoor stool much neater
The comfort from the heat indoors
Felt better to your seater!
Then the sewer system came
The answer to ground pollution
The SEWER PLANT was now the answer
To our town's B.M. solution.
We built one great big outhouse
Along the creek I think
So everyone all over town
Could share the cost and stink!!
Politics may be at fault or so the story goes
If D.E.R. is on our side
Why must we hold our nose???!!

THE HANG GLIDERS

They leap off Jacks mountaintop with cautious fear.
Their muscles strained, their faces taut.
Trusting the forces of the air that haunt,
Gravitation and its power to persevere.

Faith and courage are the tickets for their fare.
Experience is their uniform for flight.
Strength, their fellow traveler's delight,
As they catch a breath of cool fresh air.

Like giant birds of prey they glide with ease.
The currents of the air take them away.
Their minds are full of triumph as they play,
With wings that catch the strength of heaven's breeze.

Man's desire to fly will never go away.
The challenge brings to life a certain chill.
To fly beneath these wings is quite a thrill,
Then land somewhere beyond the sunset's ray!

DAVE'S BARBER SHOP

The Barber Shop in every town
Is quite a place to be around.
The sound of clippers cutting hair,
As talk of current events fill the air.
The friendly greetings at the door,
The sight of hair upon the floor.
The pleasant fragrance in the air, creates
An atmosphere for cutting hair.

I can't recall my first time there,
Or if I feared that awesome chair.
But I recall with pleasant thoughts,
The Sugar Daddys and lollipops,
He always shared with us little tots!

But time goes on and sights and sounds
Are always changing in little towns.
The people that we would often greet
Are no longer seen upon the street.
And though this life may be sublime,
We all must have our closing time.

Today he lies at rest and peace.
His struggles in this life have ceased.
In that glory over there,
I doubt he misses cutting hair.
When the history of this little town
Is talked about or written down,

I'm sure the memories will not stop,
Without the mention of Dave Bigelow's Barber Shop!

Faith

GOOD NIGHT

God paints the sunset
Across the skies
To softly sing
Its lullabies
It's time to sleep.

God made the stars
As tiny lights
To chart the roads
Across the night
For those awake.

God made the moon
To show to man
The greatness of
His glory plan
Sliver to full.

Then the dawn
God's magic wand
Makes hearts arise
And men respond
To meet their needs.

Until the lovely
Evening skies
Lures them
With its lullabies
Back to sleep.

BREATHE DEEP - John 3:8

Have you ever wondered about the air you breathe?
You never see it come, you never see it leave.
Have you ever noticed how easily it goes
Through your mouth, into your lungs, and exits out your
nose?
When the air starts moving we say it is the breeze
Moving through the maple tree, shaking all the leaves.
When its speed begins to rise it becomes the wind
Banging on the shutters and rattling the tin.
When it slows and stops, it is just the air,
There's very little evidence that it's even there!
Jesus said, "No one knows
Where it comes from or where it goes!"

THE BIBLE LADY

There's a lady in the Valley
Or so I've heard
Who is a Pro with the Written Word!
She can influence MAN
Or so they say
To spell a word in a proper way!
She takes the Bible
Or so I'm told
To prove that her wisdom is pure as Gold.
She landed a man
This is true
Married him like the Bible said to.
It is easily seen
That is a fact
She makes him REJOICE with Scriptural Tact!
Many women don't know
The SCRIPTURE they need
To capture a man so he is freed!!

HE IS RISEN

The angry mob was not sure why,
Still their cry was "Crucify!!"
Pilate said, "He's done no wrong."
Still the echo from the throng,
"Crucify!!"
Indecision at its best
Doesn't cause a crowd to rest.
Angry cries still ruled that day.
Pilate said, "Go have your way,
Crucify!!"
Still today we have a choice,
To judge him as we raise our voice.
What they didn't know back then,
Crucify was not the end.
"Crucify!!"
The empty tomb still echoes loud,
The voice of God above the crowd!
The will of God brings correction!
The voice of God, "Resurrection,
Resurrection!!"

THE "PERISH'N" GULF

In the land of the Bible's beginning
Where wars seem never to cease,
Lies a body of water that transports
Relation-ships looking for peace.

They carry the oil of "gladness"
So the lives of men can increase.
Peace in the soul is unaltered,
As relation-ships sail into peace.

Somewhere in eternity's future
Lies a gulf now empty and deep.
Relation-ships no longer sail freely,
In sorrow, the sailors now weep.

They carried the oil of "mourning,"
In agony they now despair.
They seek for one drop of water,
But the gulf is empty up there!

Relation-ships not made in heaven
Are selfish, proud and fail.
For the oil of "mourning" doesn't mix,
With the water on which they sail!

ARMCHAIR WARRIOR

I sit here in my armchair, warm,
Watching clips from Desert Storm.
Praying God, "Please bring peace
So my wallet won't decrease."
I believe in peace!

"God, please keep, guide and bless
All those fighting in this mess.
Protect their lives I pray, dear Lord,
I need gas to run my Ford."
I believe in peace!

"I know, oh, Lord, that fighting is wrong,
But prosperity keeps the U.S. strong.
Oh, how I thank you for this rest,
Please hold my name upon request."
I believe in peace!

GOD MUST SMILE

God must have smiled at Satan's doom
When the earth began to bloom.
Creating man from the dust
Free from fear, hate and lust!
Perhaps He laughed!

God must have smiled at Satan's doom
When Noah loaded the two baboons,
When God shut the loading door,
With Noah's family and with more.
Perhaps He laughed!

God must have smiled at Satan's doom
When Isaac sprang from Sara's womb.
God's promises are always sure
His intentions always pure.
Perhaps He laughed!

God must have smiled at Satan's doom,
When Christ was born, a savior whom
Would save his people in despair.
Healing them with love and care.
Perhaps He laughed.

God must have smiled at Satan's doom
When Christ arose out of the tomb.
Freeing us from Satan's power
Every day and every hour.
Perhaps He laughed!

When with our God in heaven's glory
We share again redemption's story,
Our songs of praise will not be odd
On streets of gold, instead of sod,
We'll laugh with God!

A BLESSING

May the garden of God that you walk through each day
Bring you beauty and a fragrance to brighten your way.
May the birds always sing with a melody clear.
May the presence of God always be near.

May your heart and soul always be blessed.,
Even at times when you are distressed.
Be assured as you walk on earth's sod,
You are walking in the garden with God!

RAINBOW OF LOVE

Love is like a rainbow
Arched across the sky,
Its loveliness entraps the soul
Its glory never dies!

Love is like a blossom
Pure, fresh and clean,
Showing forth its beauty
Against the budding green.

Love is like a gentle brook
Winding through the vale,
It brings refreshment to the soul
When other things would fail!

God always has a rainbow
Somewhere standing by,
He paints its lovely colors
Across the breaking sky.

True love comes from heaven
The Bible makes it known,
God has a lovely rainbow
Around His glorious throne!

THE LAME MAN

The lame man sat at the temple gate,
All he could do was sit and wait!
But something seemed special about this day.
What it was, he couldn't say.

Perhaps it was the bird on his windowsill,
As the light was breaking over the hill.
His heart had been thrilled by its beautiful song.
He had felt so sad when it had gone!

Today as usual his head was bowed,
Hoping for sympathy from the crowd.
He saw two men coming his way
He hoped, of course, it would be a good day!

It was Peter and John coming his way.
They were going into the temple to worship and pray.
Peter said, "I have no wealth,
In the name of Jesus, you can have your health!"

The lame man's face was filled with surprise.
He could move his legs and he started to rise!
In his heart great joy arose,
As for the first time he could wiggle his toes!

He went leaping and shouting as he ran,
"Praise God! I'm no longer a crippled man!"
And I heard it said the rest of the day,
"Praise Jesus, Praise Jesus," was all he could say!

BEHOLD THE WIND

If everyone could, like the wind,
Change directions from within.
Fill with fury without loss,
Then find peace at the foot of the cross!

Be impartial about a name,
Not influenced by riches or by fame.
Fill the world with awe and bliss,
Touching lives so often missed.

Leave impressions by their touch
Knowing that their life is such;
That God's love will linger on
Even after they are gone!

The wind just simply comes and goes,
It never picks friend or foe.
So God wants his love to flow,
Then everyone on earth will know!

HEAVEN IS GLORY LAND

In the beginning God made man from earthly sod
Made him a garden fair the tree of life was there
Everything there was right it was a lovely sight.
O, that was glory land.

But in that garden free was a forbidden tree
After they took a bite, nothing was ever right
It brought them to despair gone was the glory there
Gone was their glory land.

Now heaven's moved above yet God has shown his love
He sent his son to save his people from the grave
Now he is building there mansions so bright and fair
Over in glory land.

Chorus:
Heaven is glory, glory, heaven will tell the story.
Heaven is peace and love, heaven is up above
Heaven will always be part of eternity.
Heaven is glory land.

Family Memories

IN MEMORY OF GRANDMOTHER
MARY E. KANAGY
Died January 12, 1977

Grandmother, you have left us and taken your flight
To dwell in the land of peace and delight.
We'll always remember your humor and mirth
And all the kind things you've done while on earth.
No doubt as you entered through heaven's great door.
You were greeted by loved ones who had gone on before.
No doubt as you knelt down before the great throne
You hears Jesus whisper, "My Child, welcome home."
Perhaps as you stand, and look all about
You could describe to us briefly what heaven is like.
In silence we listen but nothing we hear.
And then comes the message, it's coming quite clear.
It seems you are saying, "Your minds can't contain
The glories of heaven in your mortal frame."
Perhaps with the psalmist we would hear you say,

"God's glory is shown to you every day,
Take a look at creation, the fall and the spring.
Take a look at the flowers and hear the birds sing.
Take a look at the deer as it steals through the dusk,

In search for some corn hidden under the husk.
Take a look at the bear for his search is not vain,
For honey to sweeten the lips of his frame.
Take a look at the trout as he swims in the brook,
And do not despair if he won't take your hook.
Take a look in the sky as you hear the geese call,
For it seems as they beckon the spring and the fall.
Take a look at the gold hidden under the sod,
And always remember it's put there by God.
Take a look at the sun as it sets in the west,
For by its great beauty is God's glory expressed.
Take a look at the snow as it comes tumbling down.
And with its great beauty it covers the ground.
Take a look at the moon as it shines in the night,
And always remember that God is the Light.
Take a look in the Bible for there you will find,
Peace for the soul and rest for the mind.
And always remember to look in the sky,
For the coming of Jesus is drawing nigh,
Then together forever his praises we'll sing,
As we worship and honor our Savior and King."

MEMORIES OF GRANDMA
Mrs. Amos (Mattie) Glick

As a little boy, almost every day,
I would ask to go to Grandma's to play.
After school I would always say,
"Can I go to Grandma's today?"
But mother had some work, as I might know,
She would say "Pull the weeds then you can go."
Or "Bring in the wood," Or "The grass is high."
With the old push mower I'd make it fly.

Grandma would be rocking by the window,
There she loved to sit and sew.
Most of the time she would be singing too.
I would like to share one chorus with you.
It was a song about Noah and his ark,
He chorus I still remember in part.
The animals went in two by two,
Hurrah, hurrah. The animals went in two by two,
The elephant and the kangaroo, hurrah, hurrah,
O boys, we're sailing on."

Grandma surprised me one day I was there.
She showed me the earring she used to wear.
Golden earring, what a surprise,
And her ears were pierced, I couldn't believe my eyes!
I was so surprised to say the least
The memory of those earrings will never cease!

Grandma usually had some kind of treat,
Candy, cookies or crackers to eat.
Salted pickles, from an old brown crock,
With a lid made of slate, held down by a rock.
Though knowledge increases as the mind stirs,
I have yet to find salted pickles like hers!

Time goes on, as everyone knows.
History repeats itself, the saying goes.
And usually our children ask each day,
"Can we go to Grandma's house to play?"
The answer I suppose you already know,
"Pull the weeds, then you can go."

GRANDPA AMOS GLICK

Listen, my children, and you will hear
The memories of a man whom I hold dear.
It was back sometime before the year forty-nine,
When I was knee high to a porcupine.

The home farm was thriving with cows and hogs,
And an old mean rooster that liked to flog.
The milk house was small as I recall.
The man in charge was my Grandpa.

Now Amos Glick was my idol, of course.
His transportation was by buggy and horse.
He hauled his milk to the old KaVee,
Many a day he would stop for me.

His horse was old and we traveled slow,
Most of the people we met he would know.
I rode with pride by his side on the seat.
On the way home I would get a treat!

It was quite a ride to the old KaVee.
Many a sight you no longer see.
The people I'm told would wonder of course,
Was Grandpa older, or was it the horse?

The drug store was always my favorite stop.
It was right beside the barber shop.
The ice cream he bought me filled me with pride.
The treat was always the joy of the ride!

One of the memories I ought to share
Was that sometimes I would find some hair
Come floating back from off of the horse.
It would land right on my ice cream, of course!

Grandpa was crippled and walked with a cane.
He had arthritis, it caused him much pain.
But he was rough and his skin was thick.
He never gave up until he got sick!

Yes, by the way, he had a beard.
Some would think his haircut weird.
Hard work seemed to make him tick.
But his beard wasn't as gray as his son, Willis Glick's!

The pathway of life, if you know what I mean,
Has many and various changing scenes.
For change is always found on earth's sod.
But there is never a change in our Father, God!

50 YEARS OF MARRIAGE
November 16, 1963 – November 16, 2013

This summer we had a wonderful surprise.
Our children seemed to fall out of the sky.

They took us to King's Camp for a big celebration.
We also enjoyed our grandchildren's vibration.

Our children believe their mother is the best.
They like to rise up and call her blessed.

What they call their father will do as well.
There are some things no one should tell.

We know creation's story is true.
God said it all starts when we say "I do!"

THE FIVE-LEGGED DEER

It was 2009, a wonderful year
When Jeremy shot a buck, a five-legged deer.

You should have seen the size of its rack.
No doubt the fifth leg took some weight off its back.

There is a debate about the number of points.
One Uncle said eight with two little joints.

But no one can argue the size of the deer,
Three legs in the front and two on the rear.

His Grandma Peachey said, "It's a mystery,"
For never before in all of their history

Had anyone shot this big a deer,
Three legs in the front and two in the rear.

This is a story, I guess that's clear.
Bigger lies, of course, you probably won't hear.

But his Grandpa who was tired of cutting off meat
Was sure this deer had five feet.

Now Jeremy is really a humble guy.
He's studying at college and we're wondering why.

JEREMY

He's one year old
Built close to the floor.
His words are hat
And more, more, more.

He likes his ball,
He likes to sing.
You should see him dance,
This little king!

His hair looks red,
You can tell.
This little fellow,
Is alive and well!

At Grandpa's house
He demands attention.
And other things
We won't mention!

With Uncle David,
He has things to do.
It's hard to tell
Who's spoiling who!

He's our first grandchild.
As he goes out the door,
Of course we're thinking
More, more, more.

Introspections

CAFETERIA STYLE

The world is like a cafeteria
Where we stand in line
To dish up anything we choose,
Of we think it's fine.

The choices are quite numerous.
Our tastes are so inclined,
To choose the things we like the best,
So our lives will be refined.

The church picks up the Bible,
Words of eternal life,
To guide and lead it in the way,
Of peace, instead of strife.

But in this world of choices,
Some have their own criteria.
So they use the Bible the same way,
They would a cafeteria!

FLY OR WALK?

I watched the ducks
As they flew by,
I thought,
How wonderful to fly!

To fly without a care,
Or thought,
Of what could be,
Or what is not.

For the earth would
Have no pull, you see,
On this struggling heart
Inside of me.

I'd rest at evening
Rise at dawn.
Just to do whatever
Turned me on!

If I heard
The hunter's gun,
I'd really have
A lot of fun!

I'd spin, dive,
Circle high,
Until he'd simply
Sit and cry.

I'd call to him,
You foolish man,
I fly in the heavens,
You walk on the land!

I'd call, but wait,
How would I talk?
I think perhaps,
I'd rather walk!!

I'M COMMITTED!

I'm committed to my job,
For here I make my money
I have to keep the kids in style,
Along with my dear "honey."

I have to keep the "wolf" away,
He's puffing at my door!
But, I'm so busy, I'm kaput,
There's no way I can score!

I'll never have my name in lights,
Nor ascend upon a throne.
But some day in the future,
I'll have my name in "stone."

Yes, I'm committed, and my "shrink"
Knows I'm getting bored!
He says I ought to drive a Chevy,
Instead of pushing a Ford!

FISHERMEN

Spring brings joy to fishermen
For it is time and they know when
To go and catch a nice big trout
For fishing is what their life's about.

They hope the first day will be nice.
Don't try to give them any advice,
For they will fish in snow or ice.
They are willing to pay the price.

They know their place in the human race.
Get there early if you want a space.
If you helped to stock the trout,
You know what this is all about.

They stand together side by side.
Their expertise brings them pride.
The lies they tell are always true;
They know just how to humor you.

Their many secrets you won't know
Don't ever ask them where they go.
Their answers you never can define
Cause they bait the hook and throw you a line!

BANANA SOUP

There is a racist English group,
Who never heard of banana soup.

They, of course, are always right.
To pick on the Dutch is their delight!

The way they always monkey around,
They must eat bananas by the pound!

The way they act, one might think
They all belong to the missing link!

Bananas are part of creation's story,
Why would these racists think them gory?

The Dutch will do whatever they please
And you don't have to chase them out of the trees.

I'M THANKFUL

That I could retire,
Kick up my feet and sit by the fire.
For a fine family and a very fine wife,
Who puts up with me and causes no strife.
I'm blessed with a home, a roof over my head,
Food I have plenty and just enough "bread."
For my church that teaches right and wrong.
A spiritual family that helps keep me strong.
I'm thankful for freedom. I love being free
To fly with the bird, buzz with the bee.
Race with the rabbit, dart with the deer,
Drink from a stream and know God is near!
I thank God with all my heart that he saw fit for me,
To be born in this land of America, a land that is free!

R

O

Y

If you look close enough, maybe you can tell,
This poem turned into the Liberty Bell.

THE IMMORTAL STALLION

They saw him first standing proud and grand,
Head held high checking the scents that drifted across the
land.
They saw him later on a little rise,
His silhouette against the evening sky.

This horse was strong and fearless for he knew
That all his enemies he easily could subdue.
The mares would never let him out of sight,
For their security depended on his might.

Only men brought fear within his heart
He had not liked them from the very start.
Their presence there he could not understand
Just why were they intruding on his land.

This band of men as now you might have guessed
Pursued him constantly and would not let him rest
Until at last they held him with a rope.
Then they worked until his spirit broke.

Today you'll find him standing proud and tall
Upon a monument outside of City Hall.
His silhouette still there against the sky
Reminds us of those fearless days gone by.

Upon his back there rides a famous man
Whose history is written in the books about our land.
But as I stand and watch them there, I'm wondering, of course,
Should not some recognition be given to the horse?

LIFE AND TIME

I sat upon the sands of time to think
About the days, months, years and how they shrink.
Washed away forever in the sea of life,
Some were calm, some were full of strife.

I basked there beneath the sun of happiness
And watched the sea of life regress.
Then proceeded aggressively and unafraid
To change the progress that the world had made.

I saw the castles built so strongly disappear.
I saw the people trembling in fear.
Then I saw the ruins stand,
But there was not a trace of woman, child or man.

Then I saw a little child appear,
Young, innocent and free of fear.
That child rebuilt those castles fair and grand,
Unaware of the waves that moved upon the sand.

I wonder at the mystery of life,
The rise and fall of nations, love and strife.
How birth and death open up the door
Into a land, a land we can explore.

The sands of time are shifting constantly.
They challenge people to be brave and free.
They test our faith, strength and ability to see
Beyond the ups and downs of life, into eternity.

DEATH

Death is a door that opens wide
Each of us must step inside.
Inside we'll find peace and rest
Release of the soul from this temple of flesh.
Many wonders in heaven we'll find
Wonders that boggle the finite mind!
As you sorrow for a loved one gone
Remember the joys of the great beyond.
Life is forever, death is the door
Through which we enter heaven's shore.

DEATH OF SELF IMAGE

Now they call this thing a "cough-in"
Though it never makes a sound.
They always fix it up real fancy
Though it ends up under ground.

With a little silk and satin
With a nice soft pillow too,
We can rest and be real comfy
When our life on earth is through!

It may cost a pretty penny
Or perhaps a couple grand.
We're sure to lose a lot of money
When we're buried in the land.

Each of us is born with nothing
We work for years for a buck or two.
Why spend it on a fancy coffin
When a nice pine box would do!

When my days on earth are ended
And my eyes no longer see,
If you come to see my coffin
How disappointed I will be!!

UP
AND
DOWN

Sometimes I'm happy
And laugh and sing.
Sometimes I'm angry
And hate everything
Sometimes I go forward
Sometimes in reverse.
Sometimes 'round and 'round
That's even worse.
Sometimes I hit bottom
And my life is disrupt.
Then the Lord will remind me
Unless I am down, he can't help me up!

FIRST CLASS ILLITERATES

In the corncribs of prosperity we find the dem-oc-rats,
Chewing away contentedly,
But never looking fat!

In the grain fields of prosperity we have re-pub-li-cans,
Getting drunk on profits,
Along with deep dark tans!

Then we have the menno-nites with their winning ways,
Earning a buck whenever they can,
To luxu-sure-ize their days!

Depending on the name we use,
Some will think it funny,
That we never read, "In God We Trust,"
When we count our money!

1989 YES OR NO

T'was quite a year
T'was quite a time
When freedom's bell
Began to chime.
Barriers came down
As people cheered
T'was freedom yes
As roads were cleared.

The Berlin wall
Was first to crack
As Communism gave
Some slack.
The lamps of freedom
Began to glow.
Dictators cried,
"Oh, never, no!"

T'was quite a year
As we all know
For some t'was yes
For others no.
Freedom always
Finds its place
As men run
The human race.

Freedom's voice

Will always bless
Everyone who
Answers yes.
History's words
Are to show
Why men answer
Yes or no.

FOOD FOR THOUGHT

As thoughts of men plow furrows through their minds,
They uncover dreams and wishes of all kinds.
They turn expertly out of that rich soil,
Desires for pleasure and for rest from all turmoil

Into these furrows knowledge plants its seeds,
And plants spring up to furnish all our needs.
Sometimes these plants will vanish, disappear,
For lack of knowledge poisons time with fear.

The harvest has produced for us, through time,
Inventions that improve your life and mine.
As swiftly down life's highway you may speed,
Remember knowledge will supply your need.

SETH THOMAS

Seth Thomas has a habit of hanging around,
You may find him anywhere, perhaps in town.
He is a distant cousin to Big Ben.
But I hear that their opinions differ, now and then.

It's very clear to me, through observation,
He thinks he can control the entire nation.
Into his education I have delved,
I find, He can but count from one to twelve.

Though without education or degrees,
He still controls the lives of people, with great ease.
Even kings move at his commands,
All he needs to do is move his hands.

Many men have fallen in defeat!
He has a face that's hard to beat.
He makes the ladies cry for lack of time,
To freshen up and try to look divine.

The children hesitate to stop their play,
But Mr. Thomas usually has his way.
In the early morning hours he must grin,
He knows there is no way I can win.

Yes, you can argue with a man anytime at all,
But you can never argue with Seth Thomas,
his name is on the clock upon the wall.

MY FOOD MOOD

The rhubarb grows next to the lawn
Leaves big enough to sit upon,
But when I try to eat the stem
My taste says, "Stay away from them!'

The "dandy lions" in the lawn
Really do not turn me on.
Though they're cooked with bacon bits
My taste says, "Better call it quits."

Spinach is also on my list
Of foods I easily resist.
Though Popeye gets great strength and mileage
My taste says, "Oh! Tastes like silage!"

The watermelon juicy and plump
In my throat may cause a lump.
I take a bite and then I toss it,
I'll get my water from the faucet!

Lima beans are tasteless seeds.
They may be what my body needs.
The animals can have this feed
My taste says, "Lima beans are weeds!"

Mashed potatoes, meat and corn,
I could eat since I was born.
Or if I want to please my gut,
I drive off to the Pizza Hut!!

LAUGHTER

Laughter is like a cooling breeze
on a summer day,
As it clears the smog filled air
and drives the heat away,
So laughter ripples through the air
lifting all despair,
It makes the heart beat happily
forgetting all its care,
It makes the weary bones rejoice
and fills them up with zap,
It does more for the body
than an ordinary nap,
So find a little laughter
to brighten up your way,
And you will find that life is more
than just another day!

HAPPY VALENTINE'S DAY

It's Valentine's Day, I'm sure you know
The signs are everywhere you go!
Candy hearts and cards that tell,
That Cupid is still alive and well.

Flowers play romantic tunes,
Causing lovers' hearts to swoon.
Years ago they called it spoon,
Often under the light of the moon.

But love is more than Cupid's bow,
Shooting arrows, as we know,
Though romance plays a vital part
In winning over someone's heart!

Love is sharing a lovely smile
Love is going the second mile.
Love is helping someone in need,
Love is sharing instead of greed.

Love is a mother's lullaby
Soothing her child, so it won't cry.
Love is the father giving his son,
Some of his time to have some fun.

Love is a fruit, a fruit of God's spirit.
A gift from God, you need not fear it!
He sets the heart and spirit free,
His love gives us liberty.

His love lasts the whole year long,
In every heart he puts a song.
Cupid's arrows often miss,
But God's love brings eternal bliss!

PUPPY LOVE

There's nothing like a puppy to make a boy's heart leap,
Make his eyes pop open and activate his feet.
There's nothing like a kiss from a puppy's little nose,
To make a boy feel loved regardless of his woes.

Oh, it's such a pleasure to sit upon the ground,
Let him crawl upon your lap and let him play around.
You should see his floppy ears, they nearly touch the ground,
His legs are short and thick, he's a perfect rabbit hound.

His tummy almost touches the ground as off he goes,
His tail is always wagging, he hasn't any foes.
When he runs he bounces, what a sight to see.
He's so roly-poly and as cute as he can be!

No, there's nothing like a puppy, how do I know it's true?
I was once a little boy, I had a puppy too.

THIS MONKEY BUSINESS

I saw a monkey in a tree
I looked at him, he looked at me.
It seemed together we agreed
That he was he and I was me.
But as he swung from limb to limb
I began to envy him.
It began to wonder me
If perchance it could be,
That one time I was he instead of me.
If I was he instead of me,
I wonder what happened, could it be,
That I had swung upon a tree.
Eating bananas while swinging so free?
I wonder what it could be you see,
That would have made me him, instead of me?
But now, of course, since I am me
And he still swings upon a tree
A human he can never be!
Evolution is Satan's chuckle.
For I am not a monkey's uncle.

Humanity

CLOCK NUMBER 1334

Let me tell you a story about a man named Zook,
You'll find his name in the telephone book.
If you can't tell which Zook is which,
Don't look for Urie, look for Rich!

You started in assembly, so I hear,
But made your big money in Press and Shear.
The rhythm from your money machine,
Made the inside of your wallet thick and green.

They tell me you're a man who will never crack,
Just one more knife back, one more knife back,
And when you go home and jump in the sack,
You know tomorrow it's back, back, back!

May your future be happy, your retirement be long!
May you always be right and never be wrong!

You're free now to do whatever you wish,
Watch TV, hunt or fish!

You worked in Press and Shear for ten years with few mis-
takes,
That of course, includes your breaks.
6021 is still your place
That thump, thump machine will remember your face.

Have a great time, whatever you do.
Write a story book, one that is true.
Come back to see us and tell us a joke,
We'll need the laugh, you know we're all broke!

TOOL AND DIE MEN WHO MEASURE UP

They enter their work area
Desks lined against the wall
Like the starting gate
At a horse race.

The buzzer signals the start
They move slow but sure
To accept the challenge
Of near perfection.

Like locomotives, they are
Driven by "Engineers"
Who chart the course
They must follow.

Prints become surf boards
With highs and lows
They ride the waves
Of their intellect.

These men have little tolerance
For inanimate matter
They "Stare'et" the facts
Check their micrometer.

As the metric soldiers advanced
Victory came through conversion
Perfect parts are their goal
Quality their flag of independence.

Now and then they break and flip
The loser pays for the caffeine trip
Coffee releases humor and debate
Cup in hand they return to the starting gate.

THE OTHER SIDE OF THE TRACKS

Beyond the cities' vast estates
Through the earth's wide open gate,
Another world somewhere awaits
On the other side of the tracks.

Little houses with fancy cars,
TV dishes checking the stars,
Bringing pictures back from Mars
On the other side of the tracks.

Junkyards show the aging woes
Of rust and wreckage as they pose.
Someone isn't on their toes
On the other side of the tracks.

Here the weeds and bushes hide
Buildings that have lost their pride.
What a sight for those who ride
On the other side of the tracks.

Across the waters deep and blue
The fog is thick and blocks the view.
Soon the sun will dry the dew
On the other side of the tracks.

A fleeing deer with its white tail
A cotton field along the rail,
Milk cows waiting for a pail
On the other side of the tracks.

Catfish farms for miles and miles
Done in many different styles
Bring the diner many smiles
On the other side of the tracks.

Here church steeples still arise
To pull God's love out of the skies
And free the heart from Satan's lies
On the other side of the tracks.

The train moves swiftly on the track
Undeterred by what they lack
Not everyone has turned their back
On the other side of the tracks.

FISHERMEN

Spring brings joy to fishermen
For it is time and they know when
To go and catch a nice big trout
For fishing is what their life's about.

They hope the first day will be nice.
Don't try to give them any advice,
For they will fish in snow or ice.
They are willing to pay the price.

They know their place in the human race.
Get there early if you want a space.
If you helped to stock the trout,
You know what this is all about.

They stand together side by side.
Their expertise brings them pride.
The lies they tell are always true;
They know just how to humor you.

Their many secrets you won't know
Don't ever ask them where they go.
Their answers you never can define
Cause they bait the hook and throw you a line!

Roy David Kanagy was born in 1942, and married Rita in 1963. They raised four children — Tamela, Curtiss, Robert, and David. They had ten grandchildren and five great-grandchildren. Roy worked for Ford-New Holland for thirty years and enjoyed writing poetry (which he regularly published in local newspapers), fishing, hunting, and especially time with his family.

Poem Dates

Memories of Grandma - 1978
Winter Choices - 1978
A Stable Peace - 1982
The "Perish'N" Gulf - 1990
Spring Doubts - 1992
The Bible Lady - 1994
Mary's Lullaby - 1994
Cornfields - 1994
Rainbow of Love - 1994
New Holland's Belleville Plant - 1996
Crafty Indian - 1996
The Roar of Silence in Belleville - 2007
The Light in the Stable - 2008
The Lights of Christmas - 2009
The Five-Legged Deer - 2009
Fisherman - 2010
Go Jump in a Lake - 2010
50 Years of Marriage - 2013